BASED ON REAL STORY

HUSTLE.
GRIND

LAUNCH YOUR PROFITABLE SIDE
HUSTLE AND ESCAPE THE 9-5 GRIND

A STEP-BY-STEP GUIDE TO
BUILDING YOUR ONLINE EMPIRE

WALTER STEP

TABLE OF
CONTENTS

CHILDHOOD DREAMS

How many of us, in our childhood, dreamt of reaching for the stars? How often did those innocent dreams fade away amidst the hustle and bustle of adult life, consumed by responsibilities and a job that devoured all our time? How many of us dreamt of becoming astronauts as children, yearning to gaze upon the stars and embark on fascinating journeys to faraway places? I, too, harbored such dreams, and though I did not become an astronaut, I ventured into the realm of space engineering, launching rockets and satellites into the space. Little did I know that, as the days passed, I would find myself launching online businesses instead of satellites.

Life has a way of steering us down unexpected paths, diverting us from our childhood aspirations. Yet, deep within our hearts, those dreams remain, whispering to us in the quiet moments when we dare to listen. They remind us of the limitless possibilities we once believed in and the sense of wonder that captivated our youthful spirits.

As I reflect upon my own journey, I realize that it is never too late to revive those dormant dreams, to resurrect the childlike imagination that once fueled our ambitions. The pursuit of a side hustle, an endeavor outside the realm of our 9-5 jobs, can be the key to unlocking the doors to our forgotten dreams.

In the vast expanse of the internet, a new frontier emerges, where opportunities abound and entrepreneurial spirits thrive. We can use technology to propel ourselves into a realm of boundless possibilities, just as I previously used rockets to launch myself. The online world offers a playground for innovative ideas, where passion and dedication can transform mere concepts into flourishing businesses.

It is time to shed the shackles of routine and embrace the untapped reservoirs of creativity within us. Let us embark on a journey to reignite the flames of our childhood dreams, to gaze upon the stars with a newfound appreciation, and to chart our own course in the vast cosmic sea of entrepreneurship.

In the following chapters, we will delve into the practical actions and procedures required to develop a thriving side hustle while juggling the responsibilities of our daily lives. We will investigate the power of utilizing our existing abilities and interests to create profitable online side hustles that not only give financial stability but also fill our spirits with a sense of purpose and joy.

So, let us embark on this voyage together, rediscovering the dreams that have long slumbered within us. Let us embrace the wonders of the online realm, where we can carve our own destinies and unleash our entrepreneurial spirit. The time has come to make our childhood aspirations a tangible reality, to create a life that intertwines passion, ambition, and the pursuit of our dreams.

CHAPTER 1

FROM SPACE ENGINEER TO ENTREPRENEUR. MY STORY

———————●

I come from a fairly typical background. Both of my parents have advanced degrees; mom in engineering and dad in military service.

Like most families, my family had ups and downs, but we were never poor. There was never any worry about paying the rent or putting food on the table.. Days upon days, we would spend hours outdoors with friends, playing various games under the open sky. As I grew older and started attending elementary school, my friends and I began tinkering with homemade rockets, crafted from gunpowder and whatever materials we could find, launching them in open fields. It was my first experience and introduction to the world of rocketry.

Recognizing my potential as an engineer, my parents unanimously decided that I should pursue higher education at AirSpace University, and so I did. Do I regret the six years I spent at AirSpace University? Absolutely not. It was a remarkable time that paved the way for an exciting career. After graduating, I landed a job as an aerospace engineer at a prominent company, where I spent a fulfilling eight years. Quite a symbolic number, isn't it? During my time there, I worked on various projects, including international endeavors focused on Martian exploration.

From the depths of my childhood curiosity to the heights of educational pursuits, the foundation for my passion in rocket science had been laid. As I studied the intricacies of aircraft engineering, I discovered the wonders of propulsion, aerodynamics, and celestial navigation.

Every project I worked on at the company was a stepping stone towards my dreams. Collaborating with brilliant minds, we harnessed our collective expertise to push the boundaries of aerospace technology. Whether it was designing innovative propulsion systems or developing advanced navigation algorithms, I was fortunate to contribute to projects that aimed to revolutionize space exploration.

Still, as time went on, I couldn't deny a rising yearning for more. The corporate structure and bureaucracy began to stifle my creativity and limit my ability to explore unconventional ideas. The monotony of the 9-5 routine left me yearning for a fresh challenge, a way to ignite the spark of innovation that had fueled my childhood dreams.

During this introspective time, the idea of starting a side business took root in my head.

The idea of beginning a business on the side, away from the confines of my day job, where I could put my entrepreneurial spirit to work and transform my passions into a career, really spoke to me.

I wanted to break free and go in any direction that my imagination and drive took me.

The path from aerospace engineer to online business entrepreneur may seem like a drastic leap, but as I pondered my experiences and the skills I had acquired, I realized that the fundamental principles underlying both realms were not so different. Just as rocket science requires meticulous planning, precise execution, and a bold vision to defy gravity's grasp, entrepreneurship demands calculated risks, strategic decision-making, and unwavering determination to overcome the challenges that arise.

CHAPTER 2

THE LEAP INTO ONLINE BUSINESS

The first step towards my online business journey began with a thirst for knowledge. During breaks at work, while my colleagues gathered to smoke or sip tea, engaging in idle gossip about their personal lives, I immersed myself in business literature, motivation books, and entrepreneurial wisdom. I knew I needed to act beyond reading at such instances. I had to acquire a skill that would allow me to earn income online while maintaining my regular job. And so, I ventured into the world of website building and online advertising.

By then, Mary and I had been married for two years and were expecting our first son, Mike. Our family budget was carefully planned, yet I mustered the courage to embark on opening my first online store, specializing in smartwatches. My wife supported my decision wholeheartedly, for which I am eternally grateful. Even though inventory and advertising took up most of our budget, we took the chance. (Later, I would learn about dropshipping, a different approach that would have allowed us to avoid investing heavily in inventory, but as they say, we learn from our mistakes.) At that time, right after my regular job, I would rush to the post office to ship approximately two orders per day. Yes, my website was up and running, and the ads were running too. However, a problem arose—I couldn't see the profits from this venture. Whenever our inventory depleted, I would use my own funds to reorder 50 to 100 units of the product (smartwatches, which were not inexpensive). Six months in, I switched business models. I found a supplier who was willing to ship individual units of the product directly to customers on my behalf, at wholesale prices. This model, as I later discovered, was called dropshipping.

Dropshipping opened up a new realm of possibilities. No longer burdened with the financial risks of maintaining inventory, I could focus on marketing, customer service, and growing the business. It was a game-changer, allowing me to streamline operations and alleviate the financial strain of replenishing stock. With this newfound approach, I could channel my energies towards building a strong online presence, honing my advertising strategies, and nurturing relationships with customers.

I recognize now that every step, every trial and error, helped me learn the concept of online business. The lessons learned during this period set the foundation for future success and shaped my entrepreneurial mindset. I embraced the concept of adapting and evolving, always seeking innovative solutions to overcome obstacles.

CHAPTER 3

SIDE HUSTLING WHILE WORKING 9 TO 5

After delving into the world of dropshipping and experiencing moderate daily sales, I stumbled upon another intriguing business model: art portrait studios. The idea struck a chord with both Marie and me, as it embodied creativity and artistic expression. We decided to embark on this new venture, and I began searching for a canvas printing company while also recruiting a talented graphic designer who could create digital mock-ups. We chose print-on-demand model this time, printing artworks only when clients ordered them.. Certain printing companies operate on this model. The project was captivating, and I continued juggling my regular job while fulfilling several portrait orders each day. However, over time, I realized that there were challenges in scaling this model, especially while maintaining my 9-5 job. The difficulties primarily stemmed from the extensive time commitment required for client communication, artwork revisions, and coordination with artists and production. Meanwhile, I also honed my skills in various advertising channels, including Facebook Ads. I understood that with my expertise and experience from my own projects, I could launch advertisements and create landing pages to attract potential clients. If I could generate sales in my own ventures, I could help others do the same. That's when idea to start a small marketing agency came next.

During this period, our second child, David, was soon to arrive. I made a significant life-changing decision. I invested in high-priced one-on-one training on how to start my own Social Media Marketing Agency (SMMA). Additionally, I took a long leave to care for my newborn. It was an interesting yet challenging time. For approximately two months, I immersed myself in learning the art of cold calling, client acquisition, lead generation, conducting consultations, and fulfilling service commitments. Although officially on leave, I remained technically employed.

MY SIDE HUSTLES

ONLINE STORE WITH INVENTORY

DROPSHIPPING STORE

POD CANVAS STUDIO

SMMA AGENCY

The journey into the realm of entrepreneurship intensified as I navigated the complexities of establishing an SMMA. Balancing the demands of a growing family, personal development, and professional responsibilities proved to be a juggling act. But I wanted to succeed. Armed with newfound knowledge and skills, I diligently made cold calls, honed my sales pitch, and built relationships with potential clients. It was a period of trial and error, where each setback became a lesson learned and propelled me closer to my goals.

The decision to pursue the path of an SMMA came with both risks and rewards. It allowed me to fully explore my entrepreneurial spirit while leveraging my advertising expertise. I honed my ability to identify target audiences, craft compelling ad campaigns, and deliver tangible results for clients. The satisfaction of helping businesses thrive through strategic marketing efforts fueled my passion and propelled me forward.

CHAPTER 4

EMBRACING A NEW PATH

———————————●

After a year of acquiring clients, developing advertising campaigns, and building websites and online stores, I made twice as much as my 9-5 job. For my family, I made a tough choice. I quit my eight-year job as an aerospace engineer to start an SMMA agency.

Looking back, was it necessary for me to spend six years earning a scientific bachelor's degree? Was eight years of 9-5 work necessary? No regrets. Education gave me a firm foundation and a love of technology and IT. My employment gave me time and money to create my side enterprise.

Is university degree essential? It's not. Skills and abilities rule this age of possibility. 18-year-old millionaires hire elder generations. For example, if you are interested in IT, software development, Saas development, a CS degree may be helpful.

Our planet offers many possibilities. Success is not limited to education and work. Passion, dedication, and a willingness to learn may take someone far. Whether you go to college or start a business, what matters is your dedication to personal growth and your aspirations.

I recognize that education and work experience laid the groundwork for my entrepreneurial ventures. My 9-5 job taught me discipline, tenacity, and work ethic, while my education gave me technological proficiency.

Self-education is powerful in a fast changing society. Aspiring entrepreneurs and those with a love for a field can learn and develop abilities online through tutorials, tools, and communities.

I found that formal education, continual learning, and real-world experience are key to entrepreneurial success. Today's competitive landscape rewards adaptability, foresight, and opportunity.

CHAPTER 5

WHY CHOOSE ONLINE BUSINESS?

I earn six figures now. I can run my business on my smartphone in two hours a day, eight hours a week. I occasionally use a laptop, but my freedom and flexibility are amazing. I work everywhere, but I like my home office. I enjoy watching my kids grow with my family. It wasn't always this. I spent eight years getting here.

This book will show you how to establish your own side hustle and get comparable, if not greater, results.

Building a thriving online business while working a 9-5 will be covered. I'll reveal my three-step internet empire-building strategy.

Why I choose online over local business. Online company is the safest option in today's volatile economy and planet. Loans and bureaucratic processes for location approvals and hiring are unnecessary. Solopreneurs can earn six- to seven-figures online without a large staff.

Understanding today's online business models and choosing one that fits your needs is vital. Online company strategies that need large initial investments aren't for everyone. Not all entrepreneurs start with huge investments.

SUMMARY

Launching an offline business carries significantly more risks compared to starting an online business.

CHAPTER 6

BUILDING YOUR PROFITABLE ONLINE SIDE HUSTLE - A STEP-BY-STEP GUIDE

In this chapter, I'll outline how to start a profitable online side hustle.

My system is simple and consists of three main steps.

STEP 1: FIND THE JOB AND START LEARNING

READ THE BUSINESS   MOTIVATIONAL BOOKS

STEP 2: MASTER A SKILL FOR ONLINE EARNING

START MAKING MONEY ONLINE   AND BUILD YOUR PORTFOLIO

STEP 3: CHOOSE AN ONLINE BUSINESS MODEL

START AND SCALE YOUR COMPANY

Step 1: Find a steady-paying job if you don't currently have one. Learn and absorb knowledge during breaks and free time. Dive into motivational business literature to fuel your entrepreneurial spirit.

Step 2: Master a skill for online earning. Start making money with your acquired skill and build your portfolio and case studies to showcase your expertise.

Step 3: Create your agency or choose a suitable online business model and begin building your empire.

Typically, the complete transition from a 9-5 job to the freedom of entrepreneurship occurs during Step 2 or Step 3.

For young readers who are just finishing school, Step 0 could involve pursuing a relevant higher education degree in the field you wish to further develop. For example, if you are certain about launching tech startups, obtaining an education in Computer Science (CS) would be beneficial. However, once again, this step is not mandatory.

EXAMPLE OF IT/TECH SIDE HUSTLE

COMPUTER SCIENCE DEGREE

GET STABLE   INCOME

FULL-TIME JOB

MASTER   YOUR SKILL

GET SIDE PROJECTS

LEARN HOW TO BUILD   THE SAAS AND APPS

BUILD YOUR OWN TECH STARTUP

We'll cover each stage in detail in the following chapters to help you succeed online. From preparing yourself with the right knowledge and mindset to honing your skills and leveraging them for financial gains, this chapter serves as your roadmap to establishing a thriving online side hustle.

Building an online empire takes time, focus, and perseverance. The steps outlined here are designed to provide a structured approach and minimize the risks involved in venturing into the online business world. Embrace the process, be open to learning, and let your passion drive you towards achieving your goals.

This chapter will help you start your online business with confidence, whether you're an aspiring entrepreneur seeking financial independence or a youthful mind eager to explore the digital landscape.

So, let's dive into the practical steps and strategies that will pave the way for your profitable online side hustle and propel you towards building your own empire.

CHAPTER 7

STEP 1 - WORK AND MOTIVATION

————————————●

In this step, we lay the foundation for building our online empire.

To begin, you need to find a job with a stable income that allows you to learn online earning skills during breaks from work. Most of my readers are likely already at this stage. You may be bored with your 9-to-5 job after several years. Let's look at it differently.

Use your job as a springboard, as a path to something new. Shift your mindset about it. Often, we grow to resent our workplace due to a lack of progress, prospects, or ideas for starting our own online business. We simply see it as an endless ocean, without a guiding light illuminating the path to something greater.

How do you find that guiding light? I recommend starting by reading motivational business literature and exploring online earning models to determine your optimal path forward. In the upcoming chapters of this book, we'll delve into various business models. As for motivation, I hope I have already instilled a spark of it in the earlier sections.

Begin reading business motivational books during your work breaks and after hours. Your goal is to ignite a burning desire to build your own business and attain financial freedom.

Instead of watching TV and the news, focus on consuming fresh success stories of online entrepreneurs and their case studies.

SUMMARY

In this step, we lay the foundation. The cash flow from your job will help you stand firmly on your feet and invest your spare resources into creating your online side hustle. Reading motivational business literature and exploring up-to-date success stories of online entrepreneurs, particularly young ones, will ignite a fire within you to take action.

CHAPTER 8

STEP 2 - MASTER A SKILL TO EARN ONLINE

O nce you have ignited your motivation, it's time to dive straight into learning a skill that will allow you to earn money remotely.

I recommend focusing on acquiring the following skills:

-Setting up PPC (pay-per-click) Ads, such as Facebook Ads, Google Ads, TikTok Ads

-Website and e-commerce development on Shopify

-Web design or graphic design using Figma

-AI operations: OpenAI, Midjourney. Writing texts and generating designs

-Content creation, Reels making, vertical video editing

-Building autofunnels for online courses, for example, on the ClickFunnels platform

-SEO optimization, including AI-based techniques

-Email marketing, including writing persuasive emails with the help of AI

-Developing applications or software using No-code platforms like Bubble

By skill, I mean a capability that allows you to earn money online. The client will pay you for a service. This can be considered freelancing.

Personally, I have mastered skills in ad setup and drag-and-drop building of simple e-commerce stores on Shopify.

Start taking your first orders, even if they offer modest compensation or are done in exchange for testimonials.

You can register on major freelance marketplaces and also share your skills on social media, highlighting how you can be helpful. Don't hesitate to ask your friends to repost your content.

Hone your skills, gain experience, and build a portfolio showcasing your work.

Once you have gained experience and honed your skills, you will have choices:

- Establish your own digital agency related to your skill. For example, if you have mastered ad setup, you can open an SMMA (Social Media Marketing Agency). If you have developed skills in no-code app development, you can start your own app development agency, building MVPs for startups.

- Utilize your skills to build an online business in e-commerce, online courses, Amazon FBA, POD, and more. For instance, if you specialize in running ads for e-commerce stores, you can create your own Shopify store and effectively drive sales to it using your ad expertise.

STEP 1
WORK & LEARN

STEP 2
MASTER A SKILL

CREATE AN AGENCY   UTILIZE YOUR SKILL TO BUILD
RELATED TO YOUR SKILL   AN ONLINE BUSINESS

STEP 3   STEP 3
OPEN AGENCY   OR   **ANOTHER BUSINESS MODEL**

SUMMARY

This step is about mastering a valuable skill and leveraging it to create opportunities for yourself in the online world.

CHAPTER 9

STEP 3 - CHOOSING AN ONLINE BUSINESS MODEL

I want to begin this chapter by emphasizing that choosing an online business model is not a lifelong commitment. It doesn't imply that you have to permanently commit to one particular model.

Some online business strategies are beginner-friendly, while others need sophisticated skills and large capital investments.

Therefore, I suggest starting with a beginner-friendly online business model, knowing that you can explore and adopt new models in the future.

I have decided to focus on the five main online business models:

- Digital Agency (SMMA, Design Agency, Web Development, Web3, etc.)
- E-commerce/Dropshipping
- Amazon FBA
- Online Courses/Edtech
- SaaS (Software as a Service)

Let's discuss the pros and cons of each model (see the table below)

Business Model	Initial Investments	Margin	Payment Type	Difficulty Level
Digital Agency	Low	Medium to High	Recurrent	Medium
Ecommerce / Dropshipping	Medium to High	Low to Medium	One-time	Medium to High
Amazon FBA	Medium to High	Low to Medium	One-time	High
Online Courses / Edtech	Low to Medium	High	One-time	Medium
SaaS	High	High	Recurrent	High

Digital Agency: The digital agency model is appealing due to its high margin and scalability. It requires medium to high initial investments for team building, infrastructure, and marketing. The margin is high, as revenue is generated through service fees. The scalability perspective is positive, as agencies can expand their client base and services offered. Payment types can vary, with both recurrent contracts and one-time projects. The difficulty level is medium, requiring expertise in various digital marketing aspects. Turnaround time can vary based on client projects.

Ecommerce/Dropshipping: This model offers high margin and scalability. Initial investments are low to medium, primarily focused on product sourcing, website development, and marketing. The margin is high, as revenue is generated through product sales. The scalability perspective is positive, as online stores can expand their product offerings and target markets. Payment types can include both one-time transactions and recurrent purchases. The difficulty level is medium, involving aspects such as inventory management, marketing, and customer support. Turnaround time can vary based on product demand and scaling efforts.

Amazon FBA: This business model requires medium to high initial investments for product sourcing, inventory management, and marketing. The margin is medium, as revenue is generated through product sales on Amazon. The scalability perspective is positive, as sellers can expand their product catalog and target Amazon's vast customer base. Payment types can include both one-time transactions and recurrent purchases. The difficulty level is high, as it involves competition on the Amazon platform and managing FBA logistics. Turnaround time can range from medium to long, depending on product demand and scaling efforts.

Online Courses/Edtech: This model offers high margin and scalability. Initial investments are low to medium, primarily focused on course creation, platform setup, and marketing. The margin is high, as revenue is generated through course sales. The scalability perspective is positive, as online course creators can reach a global audience and expand their course offerings. Payment types can include both one-time course purchases and recurrent subscriptions. The difficulty level is medium, requiring expertise in course creation, marketing, and online teaching. Turnaround time can vary based on course development, marketing efforts, and student acquisition.

SaaS: Software as a Service businesses require high initial investments for software development, infrastructure, and marketing. The margin is high, as revenue is generated through recurring subscription fees. The scalability perspective is highly positive, as SaaS companies can scale their user base without significant incremental costs. Payment types are recurrent, as customers pay for ongoing access to the software. The difficulty level is high, requiring technical expertise, continuous software development.

Considering the advantages and disadvantages, starting with your own digital agency appears to be the best option for beginners. It requires low initial investment, offers high profit margins, and provides monthly recurring payments from clients.

I recommend starting with the digital agency model after gaining the necessary skills. Personally,

I chose to start an SMMA agency, and I see a growing trend in this online business model.

You may wonder why I specifically recommend SMMA?

In the past, humanity pursued gold and oil. The gold and oil of our time is attention. There is an immense battle for your attention on social media platforms. Attention has become a currency.

Big tech corporations are willing to pay significant sums for the skill of capturing and retaining attention on their platforms.

This skill is the key to the future. Those who can hold attention will be handsomely rewarded.

The same applies to content creators and influencers. Platforms and social networks actively reward content creators who can captivate their audience's attention.

By focusing on the digital agency model, particularly in social media management, you can position yourself as someone who understands the importance of attention and can help businesses harness it effectively. This skill will not only benefit your clients but also open doors to numerous opportunities and financial success for yourself.

SUMMARY

Remember, the online business model you choose now is not set in stone. It's a starting point that allows you to gain experience, learn, and pivot to new models as you continue your entrepreneurial journey.

CHAPTER 10

IF YOU'VE CHOSEN
THE AGENCY PATH

In this chapter, I want to share my recommendations for growing your agency.

With the experience you gained in Step 2, you'll be able to attract clients using case studies and examples of your work.

You can reach out to potential clients through cold emails and freelancing platforms.

At the initial stage, consider hiring assistants. Use your portfolio to secure clients and delegate tasks to your assistants.

You can find assistants on freelancing platforms, but I prefer a more interesting approach—I personally train individuals in my skill set (often through paid training) and then hire them as my assistants.

Currently, there is a trend for agencies that specialize in a specific niche or direction. For example, an SMMA agency for e-commerce brands or a design agency for Web3 projects or web development MVP for startups.

This agency model has its advantages. Clients often prefer working with smaller agencies due to cost-effectiveness, focus, and better communication.

You present yourself as a private specialist with your own team, having extensive experience in that specific niche. That's how I operate as well.

Start promoting your agency on social media through personal branding and vertical videos.

Yes, that's right. The current trend is for every brand or company to have a face.

So, instead of posting generic images from the internet, show yourself on camera, create Reels, TikTok and YouTube shorts, and produce conversational expert videos.

By showcasing yourself through personal branding, you establish credibility and trust with your audience. People want to work with individuals they can connect with, not just faceless agencies.

These videos can educate, inform, and display your industry experience. Showcasing your knowledge and personality will attract potential clients who resonate with your style.

SUMMARY

Remember, in the world of digital marketing and agency services, attention is key. By leveraging social media and embracing the personal branding trend, you position yourself as an expert in your niche and gain the attention of your target audience.

CHAPTER 11

SAY GOODBYE TO YOUR 9-5 JOB

I would like to reiterate the importance of not harboring hatred towards your current job. Hatred arises from hopelessness and a lack of motivation and future plans. Your job is a launchpad.

Use it to start your own projects.

Work like you're doing it for a higher reason.

Use leisure time for self-improvement.

When should you quit your 9-5? This is subjective and depends on your specific life situation. I cannot recommend a specific moment for you to quit your job. I can only share my own experience. I quit my job and transitioned into full-time entrepreneurship when my side hustle income surpassed my job income by two-fold. I had two kids and couldn't just leave. Therefore, I needed a financial cushion.

If you live alone without family commitments, the income ratio can be 1:1. That means once your side hustle generates a consistent and recurring income equal to your regular job, you can fully dedicate yourself to your own projects. It's important to note that the side hustle income should be stable and consistent over several months to ensure a sustainable result.

Quitting your 9-to-5 involves proper planning.

These tips may help you adjust:

1. Build a Financial Safety Net: Before quitting your work, construct a financial safety net to support you during your entrepreneurial journey. Depending on your comfort level and business, save enough money for several months or a year of living expenses. Having this safety net provides peace of mind and allows you to focus on building your new venture without immediate financial stress.

2. Validate Your Business Idea:

Ensure that your side hustle or business idea has been thoroughly tested and validated. Seek feedback from potential customers, conduct market research, and refine your offering based on the feedback received. A validated business idea increases the likelihood of success and minimizes the risks associated with leaving your job prematurely.

3. Create a Transition Plan:

Outline the steps you need to take to leave your work. Set milestones and goals for your business and establish a timeline for when you expect to achieve them. This plan will provide structure and guidance during the transition period and help you stay focused and motivated.

SUMMARY

Remember, leaving your 9-5 job is a significant decision that requires careful planning and consideration. Even if quitting seems tempting, it's necessary to develop a solid foundation first.

Follow these steps to confidently enter the world of online entrepreneurship.

CHAPTER 12

THE CURRENCY OF ATTENTION

Gold and oil were once sought. These resources built enormous empires and powered industrialization. The 21st century is different. Attention is our gold and oil.

Attention is money. It's social media and online business's most significant resource. These platforms fight for your attention, and major tech companies are willing to spend a lot for it.

What is attention-grabbing? Engage, inspire, entertain, and inform. It involves providing content that makes your audience feel heard and seen. It's not just about providing amazing content—it's also about knowing these platforms' algorithms and how they determine what gets viewed and what goes buried.

Attention is the future. Holding attention will be well-rewarded. They will build large followings, start big enterprises, and change the world.

This applies to content creators, influencers, and huge tech companies. Social media platforms promote attention-grabbing content. They help creators establish their brands and audiences with tools, resources, and support.

Attention is the future currency for online businesses, content creators, and influencers. It's today's gold and oil. Let's dive in and discover the best strategies to attract attention, grow a following, and succeed online.

Big tech companies and content creators are competing for consumer attention on social media platforms at unprecedented levels. This chapter examines attention as a currency and tactics for mastering the attention economy. Attention is the key to success for business owners, content creators, and influencers.

Your Audience: Knowing your audience helps you get their attention. Audience research, buyer personas, and target demographic wants, desires, and pain points will be covered. By understanding your audience, you can personalize your material.

Create Valuable and Relevant Content: To stand out in a sea of content, create value and relevance. We'll talk about creating high-quality content that educates, entertains, or solves problems. You may become a niche authority and engage your audience by continuously providing great material.

Authenticity is scarce in the attention economy. Authenticity draws attention and builds trust. From sharing personal stories to being transparent about your journey, embracing authenticity can differentiate you from the noise and help you connect with your audience on a deeper level.

Optimize for Attention: To compete for attention, it is essential to optimize your content and strategies. We will delve into techniques for optimizing your headlines, visuals, and calls to action to grab and hold attention. Additionally, we will discuss the importance of mobile optimization, as mobile devices dominate the attention landscape.

Utilize Visual Storytelling: Visual content has a tremendous impact on capturing attention. We will explore the power of visual storytelling and provide tips for creating visually compelling content across various platforms. From eye-catching graphics to captivating videos, incorporating visual elements into your content strategy can significantly enhance your ability to capture and retain attention.

Engage and Interact: Engagement is key to maintaining attention. We will discuss strategies for fostering engagement with your audience, including encouraging comments, responding to messages, and initiating conversations. By actively interacting with your audience, you can strengthen your connection and keep them invested in your content.

Collaborate and Leverage Influencers: Collaboration and influencer marketing can be powerful tools for capturing attention. We will explore strategies for identifying and partnering with influencers in your industry, leveraging their established audience to expand your reach. Collaborative projects and cross-promotions can introduce your content to new audiences, opening up opportunities for increased attention and growth.

Analyze and Iterate: In the attention economy, data and analytics play a crucial role. We will discuss the importance of tracking metrics, analyzing data, and iterating your strategies based on insights gained. By continuously refining your approach and adapting to changes in the attention landscape, you can stay ahead of the curve and maintain a competitive edge.

SUMMARY

Navigating the attention landscape requires a deep understanding of your audience, the creation of valuable content, and the ability to optimize and engage effectively. By implementing the strategies outlined in this chapter, you can increase your chances of success in the attention economy.

Capturing attention is just the first step—sustaining it and building meaningful connections will determine your long-term success. Embrace the evolving nature of the attention landscape, stay adaptable, and consistently deliver value to your audience.

CHAPTER 13

UNLEASHING THE POWER OF YOU

Personal branding is crucial in the digital age. You need to be able to express your unique value offer and connect with your audience to succeed. A strong personal brand may help you do that by making an impact and gaining audience trust and loyalty.

In this chapter we'll discuss how to create a unique personal brand that helps you achieve your goals.

Identifying Your Voice

Finding your voice is the first step to personal branding. How do you distinguish yourself? What is your mission and values? What sets you apart from others in your niche? What do you want to be known for? You can start creating a personal brand by answering these questions.

Your Brand Story

Create your brand story after finding your voice. This story weaves together your passions, experiences, and aspirations. Your brand story should be real, moving, and inspirational.

Online Presence

Online presence is the foundation of your personal brand. You'll display your talents, establish an audience, and engage with your community there. Social media, blogs, podcasts, and more are available platforms and channels. Find the ones that match your values and aims and develop content that resonates with your audience.

Compelling Content

Personal brand content is king. Your material should be captivating, educational, and engaging. It should highlight your talents and provide value to your audience. You may gain audience trust and authority by providing content that resonates.

So, instead of posting generic images from the internet, show yourself on camera, create vertical content: Instagram Reels, TikTok and YouTube shorts. These videos can educate, inform, and display your industry experience. Showcasing your knowledge and personality will attract potential clients who resonate with your style.

By showcasing yourself through personal branding, you establish credibility and trust with your audience. People want to work with individuals they can connect with, not just faceless agencies.

Networking

Your network is crucial for personal branding. Your network can help you promote your business and find new opportunities. You may grow your audience and become a thought leader by using your network.

Success Metrics

Building a personal brand requires measuring success. You can identify what's working and what's not by measuring and analyzing your analytics. Track website traffic, email open rates, and social media interaction.

CHAPTER 14

THE ERA OF VERTICAL CONTENT

Have you noticed Instagram, YouTube, and TikTok's surge in vertical videos? These portrait-mode, bite-sized videos have swept the internet. This chapter discusses vertical videos and how they can promote your personal brand.

Rising Vertical Videos

Vertical videos have become popular due to the advent of mobile-focused social media platforms. Instagram Reels, YouTube Shorts, and TikToks all enable vertical videos.

Why do vertical videos trend? Because they're mobile-friendly. Vertical movies are immersive because most people hold their phones vertically. Vertical videos are quick and easy to absorb, making them ideal for social media's fast pace.

Vertical Videos and Personal Branding

Personal brand building using vertical videos is possible. You can get new followers and boost traffic to your website or social media channels by generating mobile-optimized expert content. Here are some vertical video tips for personal branding:

1. Give Value: Vertical videos should be valuable to viewers. This could involve giving advise, showing a new method, or sharing professional insights. By giving value, you can become a thought leader in your field and get new followers.

2. Keep it Brief: Vertical videos are quick and easy to watch. Short videos are best for engagement. Get to the point in 60 seconds or less.

3. Optimize for Mobile Viewing: Vertical videos are designed for mobile viewing. To make your material accessible to all viewers, use subtitles or captions, or use graphics and animations to make it exciting.

4. Promote Your Videos: To optimize your vertical videos' impact, promote them across all your social media channels. Your target audience is on Instagram, YouTube, TikTok, and other sites, so post your videos there. This can help grow your own brand's audience.

SUMMARY

Vertical content enhance personal branding. By providing mobile-optimized expert content, you may get new followers, increase website traffic, and become an industry authority. Remember to provide value, keep your films short and sweet, optimize for mobile watching, and promote your videos across all your social media networks. Vertical video success and personal brand success are possible with the appropriate mindset and methods.

CHAPTER 15

TURNING YOUR PASSION INTO PROFIT

After building a strong personal brand, examine monetization options to make your brand profitable. In this chapter, we'll discuss how to monetize your personal brand while providing value to your audience.

Consulting and coaching services are a popular approach to monetise your personal brand. Use your expertise to coach, advise, or guide specialty firms and individuals. Clients wanting your unique insights can receive personalized sessions, packages, or continuing support.

Online Courses and Digital Products: Sell your expertise-related online courses or digital products. Create comprehensive educational programs to teach your audience skills, overcome obstacles, or attain goals. Create valuable, passive income-generating video tutorials, e-books, templates, or membership sites.

Conferences, industry gatherings, and workshops: Use your personal brand to get speaking gigs. Earn money by speaking to live audiences. You can also host workshops or seminars to provide in-depth training or specialized expertise to a chosen group.

Affiliate Marketing: Become an affiliate marketer for brands that match your personal brand. Promote their products on your website, social media, or content and get paid for each sale or referral. Choose audience-friendly products and be transparent about affiliate connections.

Sponsored Content and Brand Collaborations: Your own brand may attract sponsorships and brand collaborations. You may be paid to promote brands to your audience. Keep sponsored material transparent and make sure collaborations line with your values and benefit your audience.

Public Speaking Engagements: Speak at non-industry gatherings to increase visibility. Consider speaking at universities, business associations, or professional organizations. Public speaking boosts credibility, network, and income.

Brand licensing: Consider licensing your personal brand for goods or product collaborations. Branded gear, accessories, and stationery allow your audience to support your brand while generating additional cash. Ensure your products represent your brand's quality and ideals.

Sponsored Social Media Content: As a niche influencer, marketers may pay for sponsored social media content. Create compelling articles, videos, or tales about their products or services to increase your social media following and revenue. Keep sponsored material real and relevant to your company and audience.

SUMMARY

Your expertise, values, and audience's demands must guide your personal brand monetization strategy. Try multiple revenue streams, monetization tactics, and evaluations. Prioritize audience value and personal brand authenticity.

With the correct strategies and perseverance, you can build a profitable personal brand. To monetize your personal brand, be flexible, innovative, and in tune with your audience.

CHAPTER 16

INVESTING IN YOUR EDUCATION

⎯⎯⎯⎯⎯⎯●

In the ever-changing world of online business, education is crucial. In today's fast-paced market, staying on top of industry trends and best practices is essential.

Attending seminars, workshops, and courses to improve your skills are all methods to invest in your education. Investing in yourself opens doors, boosts earnings, and positions you as a thought leader.

This chapter discusses the value of education and how to stay current with industry developments and best practices.

Follow Industry Trends: To stay competitive in internet company, you must follow industry trends. To stay current, read industry journals, follow thought leaders on social media, and attend conferences and seminars. Staying updated lets you spot opportunities, predict changes, and adjust your strategy.

Seminars and workshops are great ways to learn from professionals and obtain market insights. Attend specialty or industry events to learn and network. Many seminars and workshops offer hands-on training and practical advice to build your business.

Courses: Take classes to improve your skills. Choose hands-on, niche-specific courses. Online courses allow for self-paced learning. Education opens doors and boosts earnings.

Mentors can help you navigate internet business. Ask industry leaders for advice. Respect their time and provide value for mentorship. Experts can help you improve your approach.

Join Masterminds: Mastermind groups boost learning. Like-minded people gather often to share insights, feedback, and support. Mastermind groups offer a community of peers who may provide comments and advise.

SUMMARY

Online business is constantly changing, thus investing in your knowledge is crucial. Staying current with industry trends, attending seminars and workshops, enrolling in courses, seeking mentors, and joining mastermind groups can improve your expertise, extend your capabilities, and open new doors. Invest in yourself—you're worth more.

CHAPTER 17

THE POWER OF MENTORSHIP

Online business success requires education. Mentorship can also boost your development. The appropriate mentor can help you achieve your goals and dreams.

This chapter discusses mentorship and how to locate the proper one for your internet business. We'll also examine how one-on-one training with a mentor can boost your skills.

Mentorship Matters: Mentorship boosts development. Online business mentors can offer advise and perspective. They can provide industry insights, strategy feedback, and assist you overcome issues. During difficult times, a mentor may encourage and soothe you.

Mentor Selection: Success requires finding the appropriate mentor. Search for industry leaders. Find mentors with relevant case studies and hands-on assistance. A mentor who earns at least 2x more than you has the abilities and experience to assist you reach your goals. Find mentors that share your beliefs and vision and are eager to help you progress.

One-on-One Training Benefits: Mentoring can greatly improve your talents. This method gives you personalized feedback to improve and learn new abilities quickly. Personalized counsel from a mentor can help you overcome challenges and succeed faster.

Saving and Educating: Mentorship benefits your education and future. Mentorship might be worth the first cost. By saving and investing in your education, you can succeed faster.

SUMMARY

Online business mentorship is powerful. Finding the proper mentor, engaging in one-on-one training, and saving for college can help you progress faster and achieve your goals. In fast-paced online business, mentorship is essential.

CHAPTER 18

NURTURING A GROWTH MINDSET

Growth or stagnant mindset? This question can determine your success and potential. In this chapter, we'll discuss growth mindset, why it matters, and how to cultivate it for success.

Growth Mindset—what is it?

A growth mindset is the concept that hard work, dedication, and persistence may improve intelligence and abilities. Growth-minded people see challenges and setbacks as opportunities to learn and progress. They accept criticism and take risks to succeed.

Those with a fixed mindset think their intelligence and abilities are unchangeable. They avoid feedback and are risk-averse because they see challenges as signs of their limitations.

Why Growth Mindsets Matter

Personal and professional success requires a progressive mentality. progress-minded people are more robust, adaptive, and receptive to learning and progress. They can handle disappointments and persevere better. A growth mentality also encourages risk-taking and progress.

Growth Mindset Development

Developing a growth mentality takes time, but it pays off. Growth mindset strategies:

Accept Failure:

Growth attitude requires embracing failure. Failure can be a chance to learn and improve. Analyze your failures and find ways to improve.

Study:

A growth mentality also requires learning. Focus on learning and growth rather than outcomes. Set ambitious goals, seek criticism, and try new things to learn.

Accept Challenges:

Growth attitude requires embracing obstacles. Embrace adversities as learning opportunities. Try new things, tackle new projects, and discover new interests.

Positive Thinking:

A growth attitude requires positivity. Focus on possibilities rather than constraints. Gratitude, positive self-talk, and visualization can improve your outlook.

SUMMARY

Success in life and work requires a progressive attitude. You can build a growth mindset that will help you attain your objectives and potential by embracing failure, learning, difficulties, and positivity. Remember, hard work can achieve anything. Keep learning, improving, and striving to be your best.

CHAPTER 19

BUILDING YOUR TEAM

To manage activities and expand your online business, you need a reliable team of assistants.

Consider hiring assistance to help you handle chores when starting your business. You may focus on your key strengths and build your firm more efficiently. By delegating duties to your assistance, you can focus on what matters most.

Freelance platforms can help find the team members. You can connect with freelancers from across the world on platforms like Upwork and Fiverr. Hire people for specific jobs or projects and pay them per project or hour.

However, I like teaching others in my skills and then recruiting them as assistants. I can establish a team of people who share my values and are devoted to my business's success using this method.

I hire folks who love my industry and want to learn. I hire the top performers from my paid training programs. I can establish a talented, motivated, and dedicated team using this method.

Find people that match your beliefs and vision when constructing your dream team. Look for folks who love your sector and work hard. Set clear objectives and goals and offer them the resources and support they need to achieve.

In this chapter, we'll discuss ways to establish your dream team, including hiring the proper helpers, allocating responsibilities, and developing a healthy and collaborative workplace.

Assistant Selection: The appropriate helpers are essential to developing your dream team. Look for industry enthusiasts who want to learn. Connect with specialists on freelancing sites. You may also offer paid training programs to teach others your skills and then hire the best as your assistance.

Delegating Tasks: Effective work delegation is essential for team management and business growth. Give your assistants the tools and support they need to succeed. Use project management tools to track progress and offer advice.

Creating a Supportive and Collaborative Work Environment: Building a dream team requires a supportive and collaborative workplace. Offer professional development and open communication. Create a culture of continual improvement by celebrating achievements and learning from setbacks.

SUMMARY

Building your dream team is essential to online company success. Finding the proper helpers, distributing jobs well, and building a friendly and collaborative work atmosphere can help you expand your business and achieve your goals. Your team is an extension of your vision and beliefs, so recruiting the right individuals is important to your success.

CHAPTER 20

HOME OFFICE SETUP

Isn't working from home a dream? No commutes, dress codes, or office politics. Your schedule, jammies, and breaks are up to you.

Is working from home worth it? In this chapter, we'll discuss working from home's merits and cons and offer home office setup advice.

Work-from-Home Benefits

1. Flexibility: Working from home offers great flexibility. Work when and where you choose. You can take breaks and work when you choose.

2. Cost Savings: Working from home saves money. Transportation, work clothes, and food are free. Over time, this saves a lot.

3. Productivity: Many people work better from home. Without office distractions, you can focus better and work faster.

Work-from-Home Drawbacks

1. Isolation: Working from home can be lonely, especially for team players. You may miss office companionship.

2. Distractions: Working from home is less distracting than working in an office, but there are still enough. Work might be distracted by family and household tasks.

3. Lack of Boundaries: Working from home makes it hard to separate business and personal life. Work might consume you outside of business hours, causing burnout and stress.

Home Office Setup Tips

1. Create a Home Office: A home office helps you stay focused and productive. This should be a peaceful place to work.

2. Buy Ergonomic Furniture: Your home office should be comfy. For long-term comfort, get a comfortable chair, desk, and other furniture.

3. Set Family Boundaries: If family members are at home while you work, set boundaries. Tell them your work schedule and ask them to respect it.

4. Take Breaks: Working from home can be appealing, but you should take breaks. Take a walk, stretch, or snooze to refresh.

Don't Believe the Hype - Working on the Beach is Bad.

We've all seen influencers working on the beach with laptops on Instagram. However, beach work is a bad idea. Sand, water, and beach distractions can damage your laptop. If you want to succeed, work from home or a dedicated workstation.

SUMMARY

Working from home is a dream, but it's hard. Understand the pros and downsides of working from home and set up a successful home office to maximize this opportunity. Working from home requires balance, boundaries, breaks, and focus. Remote workers can succeed with the correct mindset and methods.

CHAPTER 21

OVERCOMING DOUBTS

In the beginning of my online side hustle journey, my self-doubt grew like weeds and threatened to suffocate my dreams. My family and friends seemed to be against my aims, throwing doubt on its basis. Their words were full of skepticism, trying to bring my lofty objectives down to earth.

I wasn't going to let their mistrust break me.

I realized that these doubters were just projecting their fears and limitations onto me. Because they were locked in habit and routine thinking, they couldn't understand my audacious aspirations. They shot arrows at my determination with their comments. But I protected myself with unwavering faith, knowing I was on the correct path.

I embraced this as a challenge to do something unexpected and surprising instead of giving in to self-doubt. My insecurity motivated me to succeed. I was fueled by those who didn't believe in me.

During this life-changing trip, I developed self-confidence. Before winning over skeptics, I had to win over myself. I began a voyage of self-discovery to clear up years of misunderstanding. I found a treasure trove of latent skill in my interests.

I was surrounded by dreamers and risk takers who shared my belief that anything is possible. We formed a group of rebels because we wanted things done differently. My uncertainties vanished like smoke in the breeze when I was around them.

I heard hope after learning to ignore self-doubt. I become an expert by practicing. Each difficulty was a lesson, each setback a step forward. I was able to move forward with confidence after realizing that my self-doubt was a result of social pressures.

My critics became my biggest fans as my side hustle grew. And I became an example of the God-given potential that lives in ALL Of Us.

I offer some recommendations for those launching online side businesses: Accept uncertainties as development opportunities. Be with individuals who inspire you and bring forth your best. Believe in yourself; other people's doubts can't influence your future.

Not everyone can be an entrepreneur. Faith, tenacity, and the fortitude to reject criticism are essential. However, uncertainty diminishes and opportunity opens up as one advances. Enjoy the ride—only by addressing and conquering your anxieties can you realize your potential.

Position yourself as someone who follows their ambitions regardless of skepticism. Your actions will speak louder than the world's doubts, so follow your dreams.

CHAPTER 22

SURROUND YOURSELF WITH GOOD PEOPLE

You resemble your five closest friends. This statement is spot-on for online company growth. Supportive people help you achieve goals, stay motivated, and overcome challenges.

What does "positive influences" mean? How do you find the most helpful people? In this chapter, we'll cover the value of good influences and how to build meaningful relationships that move you ahead.

Who Are Good People?

Good people support your mission and values. A great buddy pushes you to grow and learn and supports you no matter what. There are decent people everywhere.

Why Positive Company Culture Matters

Life success requires a solid support network. Good people aid and inspire when you need it most. They may support your goals, challenge you, and hold you accountable.

How to Meet Good People

Building lasting relationships with decent people takes time and effort, but the return is worth it. Below are ways to connect with decent people.

Set Goals and Values

Clarifying your values and future ambitions is the first step to meeting great individuals. Your core beliefs? What are your self-improvement goals? Answering these questions can help you find people who share your beliefs and can help you reach your goals.

Network:

Networking events help you meet new people. Be friendly at industry events. Ask questions and look for ways to help others in conversations.

Join Masterminds.

Mastermind groups help you meet like-minded people. Like-minded people gather often to share insights, feedback, and support. Mastermind groups offer a community of peers who may provide comments and advise.

SUMMARY

Life success requires a solid support network. By defining your principles and vision, networking, joining mastermind groups, volunteering, and being a decent person, you can build strong, supportive relationships with others who can help you achieve your goals. Relationships are worth the time and effort. Find your tribe and surround yourself with nice people to help you realize your dreams.

CHAPTER 23

WHAT'S NEXT?

The process never stops; it keeps evolving. You mustn't stand still. You should always be learning something new. Successful individuals embrace continuous learning, constantly seeking knowledge and growth.

Don't waste time watching TV, playing computer games, or going to bars. Spend your time on things that will help you instead.

Online business is incredible. It's fascinating. New online business models are worth investigating, but first research them.. However, avoid jumping from one business model to another, as it leads to lack of focus and ultimately yields poor results in your primary endeavor.

Don't be afraid to invest in your education, especially when an experienced expert offers case studies and practical skill training, such as "How to Set Up Facebook Ads." I highly recommend even seeking one-on-one mentorship with a guarantee of tangible results. Although this format of learning is usually more expensive, it provides the greatest value and ensures your success.

Stay updated with industry trends, attend seminars and workshops, and enroll in courses that deepen your expertise and expand your capabilities. You're worth more when you invest in yourself.

YouTube and other platforms offer free skill tutorials, but you may have to experiment owing to the availability of material.

Read motivational business books, watch practical video tutorials that teach you new skills online, or listen to stories of successful entrepreneurs.

Begin investing your surplus funds not only in your education but also in other assets. Allocate at least 10 percent of your monthly income to investments such as stocks, real estate, or even crypto, depending on your risk tolerance and long-term financial goals. Consult financial counselors or specialists to help you invest wisely.

Mistakes I encountered along the way:

- Trying to do everything by myself and not seeking assistance from others.

- Succumbing to perfectionism, spending too much time perfecting my website or design instead of starting to acquire clients.

- Fearing the right time to raise prices and hesitating to increase service fees as my experience grew, afraid that clients might not agree to the new rates.

- Immersing myself entirely in client projects and neglecting the development of my own projects and personal brand.

To prevent burnout, here are some tips:

1. Prioritize Physical and Mental Well-being:

Engage in sports, warm-up exercises, and take walks in the park. Physical activity helps rejuvenate your body and mind, improving focus and productivity. Incorporate regular exercise into your routine to maintain a healthy work-life balance.

2. Indulge Yourself Occasionally:

Allow yourself to enjoy delicious meals at restaurants or cafes as a treat for your hard work. This small luxury can serve as a reward and motivate you to keep pushing forward.

3. Rest and Travel:

Take time to rest and recharge. Plan vacations or short getaways to explore new places, experience different cultures, and gain inspiration. Traveling can broaden your perspective and infuse creativity into your work.

SUMMARY

Doubts and challenges are inevitable on the path to success. Embrace them as opportunities for personal growth and learning. Concentrate on your goals and develop yourself.

You'll be better prepared for the future if you prioritize your health, stay happy, and seek balance.

CHAPTER 24

WHERE I AM NOW AND WHAT I'M DOING

———————●

Currently, I continue to run my SMMA (Social Media Marketing Agency) in multiple niches while also writing books. It's a fulfilling journey that allows me to combine my passion for entrepreneurship and sharing knowledge with others.

I'm taking the next step in my entrepreneurial adventure. I have a burning desire to venture into the world of software startups, specifically in the Saas (Software as a Service) niche. The prospect of building a tech startup excites me, and I believe that my past experiences and skills in online business will serve as valuable assets in this new endeavor.

We have been able to travel the world because to my 'work-from-anywhere' online business. My two sons are attending school remotely, allowing us to explore new places and cultures together. My amazing wife, Mary, is pursuing her own passion and purpose, finding fulfillment in her chosen endeavors.

Perhaps, as I walk down a street near you, we might cross paths. I am just an ordinary person who once had a big dream of reaching for the stars and, with the arrival of my family, extending those stars as gifts to my loved ones.

AFTERWORDS

The online business industry is full of ups and downs, obstacles, and achievements. Moving forward, learning, taking action, and hustling for your dreams is the key. Ignore the doubters; they can't understand your fire.

Remember that the road to success is winding. Learn from your mistakes, embrace the process, and adjust. As you manage internet entrepreneurship, stay committed, focused, and willing to change.

I'd want to thank the reader for following me on this book's trip. I hope it motivates you to become an online entrepreneur.

Now make your imprint on the globe. Embrace the Hustle, Grind, and entrepreneurial spirit.

Best wishes on your entrepreneurial journey!

GLOSSARY

AI: A computer science field that tries to construct intelligent machines that can write blog posts, recognize speech, make decisions, and solve problems.

Amazon FBA: Sellers advertise their products on Amazon, and Amazon handles warehousing, packaging, shipping, and customer service. Entrepreneurs can sell their items using Amazon's huge client base and logistics network.

Autofunnel: A marketing automation technology that automates lead generation, nurturing, and conversion. Businesses may optimize customer journeys and automate marketing using it.

Dropshipping: An e-commerce business concept without inventory. When a consumer orders, the seller buys the product from a third party and ships it. This frees up entrepreneurs to focus on marketing and customer acquisition.

Ecommerce, or Ecom, is online buying and selling. Online marketplaces or websites are used to execute business transactions. Businesses and consumers benefit from ecommerce's worldwide reach and convenience.

Edtech: Educational technology. It includes digital tools, platforms, and apps that aid education.

Figma: A cloud-based design tool for UI, prototypes, and collaborative design projects. Designers can work in real time, share design files, and collaborate on projects with Figma.

Freelance: Working for clients or companies on a contract basis. Freelancers don't have long-term contracts. Writing, design, programming, marketing, and consulting are often their specialties.

Influencer: A person with a large following. Influencers can change followers' opinions, actions, and purchases. Brands work with influencers to reach a specific audience.

MVP: Minimum Viable Product. It has the key features and functions needed to satisfy early clients and gather feedback for further development. Entrepreneurs can validate their product idea, gain user insights, and iterate depending on customer input with an MVP.

No-code: A software development approach or platform that lets people create apps and software without writing code. No-code tools allow non-coders to build and edit apps with a visual interface and drag-and-drop capability.

Pay-per-click Ads or PPC: Online advertising that charges advertisers per click. It's utilized in search, social, and display ads. Businesses can use PPC advertisements to deliver targeted traffic to their websites or landing pages and just pay for clicks.

Print on Demand (POD): A business concept where things like t-shirts, mugs, and books are made following an order. This removes upfront inventory and reduces the risk of unsold products. Print on Demand solutions allow entrepreneurs to design and sell personalized products without inventory management or fulfillment.

Reels: A social media function, especially on Instagram, that lets users create and share short videos. Reels might feature entertaining skits, lessons, behind-the-scenes footage, or brief instructional pieces and are usually 15 to 60 seconds long. Reels can be enhanced with music, text overlays, and artistic effects. Users can display their work with this feature.

SaaS: Software-as-a-Service. It's a software distribution strategy where cloud-hosted apps are accessed online. Users use SaaS apps through web browsers instead than buying and downloading software on their devices. SaaS offers firms scalable, affordable, and easy-to-use software.

SMMA: Social Media Marketing Agency. It develops and implements social media marketing strategy for clients. Content, social media, advertising, influencer marketing, and analytics are SMMA services. SMMA providers assist businesses grow their social media presence to reach their target audience and meet marketing goals.

Web3: The next generation of the internet decentralizes online interactions and gives users more control over their data and digital identities. Blockchain, cryptocurrency, and DApps build a more open, transparent, and user-centric internet economy. Web3 promotes peer-to-peer connections and user empowerment.

www.ingramcontent.com/pod-product-compliance
Lightning Source LLC
Chambersburg PA
CBHW070805220526
45466CB00002B/549